UNDERNEATH THE GOOBERRY BUSH

Poems & Drawings by

Ken Higginson

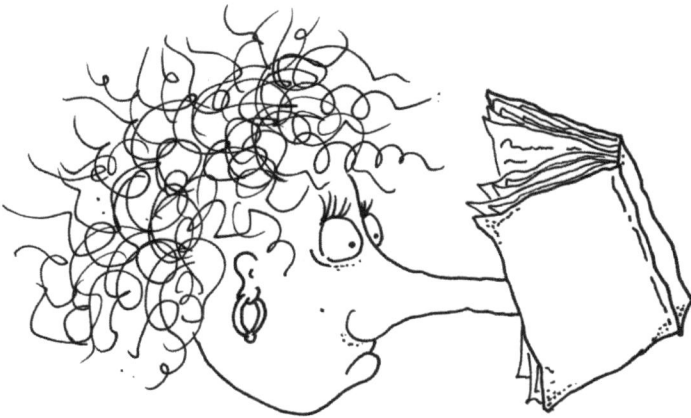

Paper Crown Studios

Printed in the USA
First Printing: August 2015
Paper Crown Studios

www.PaperCrownStudios.com   ISBN- 978-0-692-51250-0

For Isaac, Ashley, Kyle, & Ernie

Ken Higginson

UNDERNEATH THE GOOBERRY BUSH

REMEMBER

Remember the howl of the moon howlers,
The land of the princess towers,
The smell of the wishing flowers.

Remember the spells of the magic-spell speakers,
The breath of the fire breathers,
The treasure of the goblin-gold seekers.

Remember the secrets of old dusty cellars,
The riddles of the riddle bearers,
The stories of the story tellers.

PICKPOCKET

There is a sneaky pickpocket
Picking pockets in Pilfery Park.
You'll never see him coming.
He'll snatch your pockets in the dark.
He won't just take the things inside,
Like your wallet, keys, or locket.
He uses little scissors and
Takes the whole darn pocket.
So when you go and reach into it
To get your coins to spend,
Your hand will just go right on through it
And out the other end.

READY, SET, GO!

The Great Snail Race will now begin.
Who will win?
Oh, who will win?
If you really want to know, my dear,
Please come back some time next year.

HUNGRY COUCH

This couch just ate my little brother—
Swallowed him up whole.
I heard a gurgling, gulping sound.
Oh what a way to go!
He used to play with all my toys.
He used to make a lot of noise.
He pulled my hair and threw a fit.
He took my dolls and drooled and spit.
This couch just ate my little brother.
What a tragedy.
He must not have known how dangerous
A hungry couch can be.

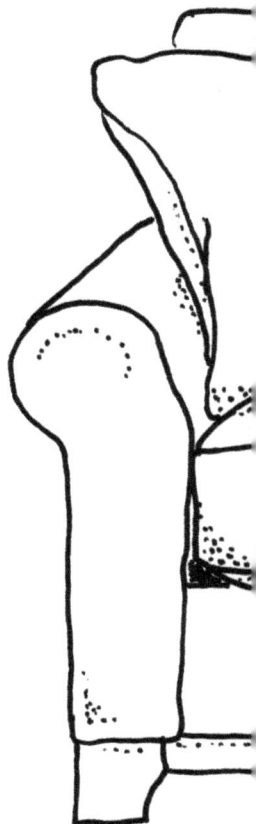

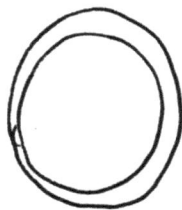

WISHES

If you make your wishes with birthday candles,
You'll get one wish this year.
If you wish upon a falling star,
You must wait for one to appear.
If you make your wishes with dandelions,
You might search and search all day.
If you buy your wishes in wells or fountains,
How much are you willing to pay?
If your wishes come from leprechauns,
You must catch one with great speed.
But if you get your wishes
From breaking Mother's dishes,
Then you'll have all the wishes you need.

THE KING WITH A PAPER CROWN

Why does the king ride a small, lowly mule?
Does it not make him look just a bit like a fool?
>His people were hungry, with little to eat,
>So the king gave his horses to plow and grow wheat.

Why does the king wear rags and not robes?
A king should look noble, as everyone knows.
>The winter was harsh and his people were bare,
>So he gave them his gowns and warm coats to wear.

Why does the king wear a crown made of paper?
Won't they think him a fraud and call him a faker?
>His people, they wanted to learn skills and knowledge,
>So he used all his gold and built them a college.

Why do the people cheer, "Long live the king"?
He has not a horse, a crown, or a ring.
>What makes a king noble isn't riches or treasure,
>But showing his people a love without measure.

GOOBERRIES

Underneath the gooberry bush
I saw some old troll toes.
I suppose a troll was strolling through
Picking berries for his stew,
Then had to leave in such a rush
He left his toes down in the brush,
Underneath the gooberry bush.

RAINBOW IN A BOTTLE

I found a glowing rainbow
And knew it would not stay,
So I put it in a bottle
To use another day.
I shared the Yellow with a lad
Who seemed a little down.
The Green was spread for luck
And fortune all around the town.
I gave the Orange to a bird
To build a feathered nest
And poured the Red onto a rose
To help it look its best.
I mixed the Purple in a bowl
To bake a purple pie,
Then let the Blue just float away
Back into the sky.

SCISSORS

Never run with scissors!
You know this is the rule.
Never run with scissors
At play, at home, or school
Unless you're being chased
By angry, wild roses
Who want to use your scissors
To cut off your fingers and toeses
And trim up your hairs
And shear off your ears
And clip off your sniffling noses.
Then run with your scissors
Held tight in your hand.
Yes, run with your scissors
As fast as you can!

CAMBRIDGE COURT

The gentlemen of Cambridge Court
Wear cats instead of hats—
One tips his cat to the other and says,
"Meow do you do today, good sir?
Meeeeow do you do today?"
The other tips his cat politely back
And says, "Quite purrrfectly,
Thank you."

HONEY BEAR

Honey Bear
Likes to scare
The birds and bugs and bees.

He roars and growls,
Laughs and howls,
And shakes the forest trees.

But when he eats
His honey sweet,
He eats it all alone.

'Cause no one cares
To be with bears
Who mumble, mope, and moan.

FUDDLE PUDDLE

Frank McFuddle found a puddle
Struggling to survive.
So he did what he could,
As any boy would,
To keep the puddle alive:

A cup of snow,
Five drops of rain,
Shade each sunny day,
A shower every April,
A bath each time they played.

Frank's puddle grew for seven years,
And then for goodness' sake,
That thirsty little puddle
Became a big blue lake.

With many years of care and love
Frank's lake grew even more,
Until one day he found himself
Upon an ocean shore.

WORKING

Hammer nail.
Hammer nail.
Hammer nail.
Hammer nail.
Hammer nail.

Faster!

Hammer nail,
Hammer nail,
Hammer nail,
Hammer nail,
Hammer nail.

Faster!

Hammer nail
Hammer nail
Hammer nail
Hammer thumb

OUCH!

Missing

There was a monster on this page
That would have made you shout.
It was smelly and scary,
Hungry and hairy,
With an ugly, slimy snout.
But when you opened up this book
Everything inside here shook,
And the monster that was on this page
Fell out.

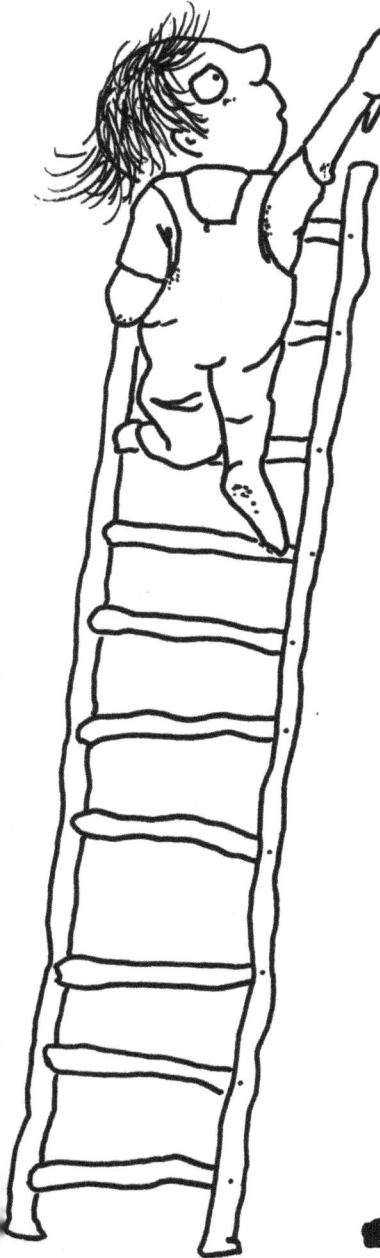

CHIMNEY TOWN

I hear there's an awful giant around
Somewhere right here in Chimney Town.
Giants, you know, really aren't half bad
'long as nobody foolish goes makin' them mad.
'n fact, the only difference from you and me
Is that their nose looks just like a chi-mn-ey.
Other than that, they're bigger of course,
Mighty cranky, and strong as a horse.
They especially don't like to be disturbed in their sleep.
Well, enough of my stories; I've got chimneys to sweep.

JOHNNY APPLESEED

Johnny, Johnny
Ain't got money,
Thinks that rich folks all dress funny,
Says that nature's all he needs
And a pocket full of apple seeds.

Johnny, Johnny
Ain't got a home,
Travels the country all alone,
Spends his days roaming free,
And sleeps beneath an apple tree.

Johnny, Johnny
Ain't got a wife,
But he'll keep lookin' all his life
For a girl who loves to make
Steaming cider and apple cake.

Johnny, Johnny
Ain't got much.
He hasn't use for things and such,
But Johnny's happy as you or me
When he plants an apple tree.

CAMOUFLAGE JACK

Camouflage Jack could not be seen;
Lyin' on grass, he'd turn himself green.
Up in a tree or down in the brush,
He looked like the leaves
Or some brush mush.

When he jumped in the river water,
He looked just like a river otter.
In a snow storm he turned snowy white,
And midnight blue in the dark of night.

He blended right into everything, that
Camouflage Jack who could not be seen.
Then Jack fell asleep atop an apple barrel,
And along came a giant named Hungry Herald.

And poor, poor, little Camouflage Jack
Looked just like Herald's favorite snack.
Down went those apples in one big bite,
Down the giant's hatch and out of sight.

Oh where, oh where did little Jack go?
Has anyone seen him?
Does anyone know?

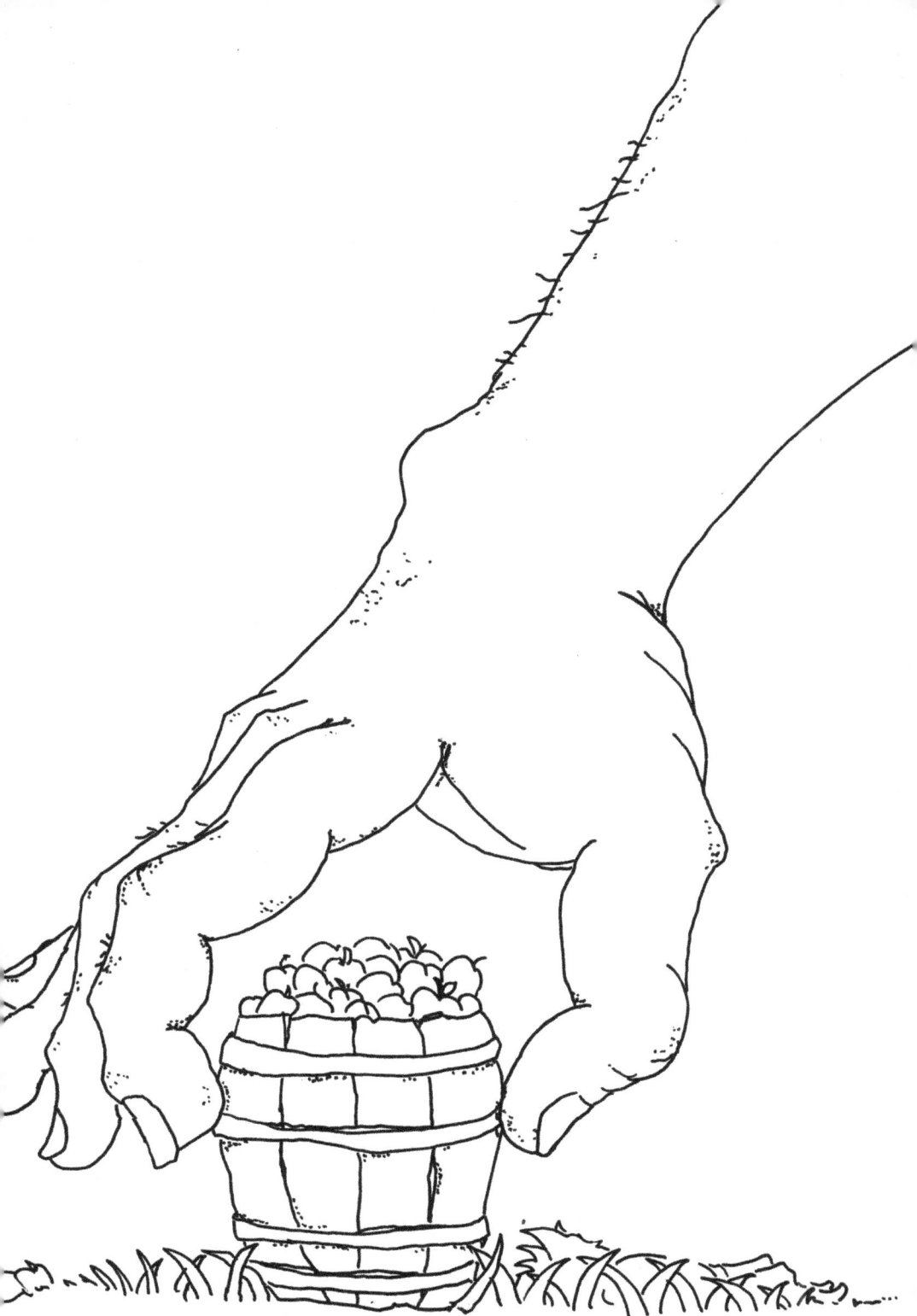

DIRT BUG DOUG

I'm digging a hole to China today
"That takes a long time," I hear you say,
But I will dig there anyway.

It might take hours
It may take days,
To dig so very far away.

Weeks will go by
And maybe years,
Could be 87 years.
Then out I'll dig with a long grey beard.

Out into a strange and curious land
With magical sounds from a Chinese band,
Of pointed hats and bamboo houses,
Of Chinese cats and Chinese mouses,
Of scented winds and golden fields,
Of statues armed with swords and shields,
Of flowing streams and endless fountains,
And pink sunsets over Chinese mountains.

You'd like to help, I hear you say.
Grab a shovel and come this way.
We're digging a hole to China today.

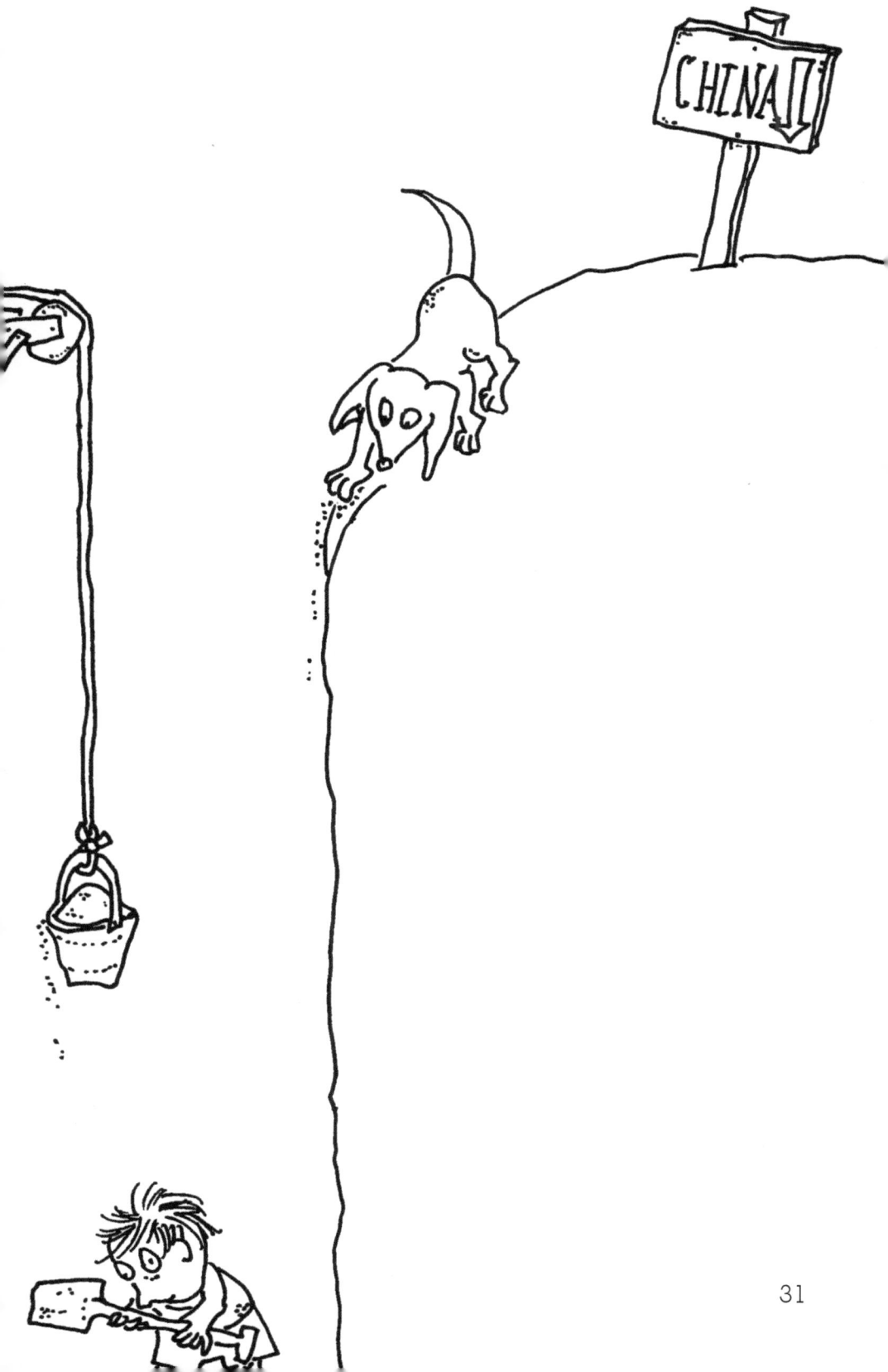

31

I'VE NEVER EVER

I've never been to Wonderland
'Cause I'm afraid of fallin'.
I've never been to Neverland
'Cause flyin' ain't my callin'.
I've never been to Camelot—
I won't get in the saddle—
Nor paddled up the river Thames
'Cause I refuse to paddle.
I've never been to Dreamland
'Cause I'd rather stay awake,
Nor spoken to a magic mirror
For fear that it might break.
I've never been to Oz—
I hide when there's a storm—
Nor crossed the vast Sahara
'Cause the desert is too warm.
I've never seen Atlantis
'Cause the journey's wrought with peril,
Nor toppled o'er Niagra Falls
'Cause I won't get in a barrel.
Perhaps I've lived a good long life
'Cause of what I've never done.
But, my dears, these long safe years
Were never any fun.

CAT-A-PULT

In days of old the cat-a-pult
Was used to siege and cause tumult
By launching cats o'er castle walls
To make a warring
Cat-a-brawl.

The cats would land
(On their feet of course),
Then go to every man and horse
And snarl and hiss
And scratch and bite
In a raging, furry
Cat-a-fight.

Hail the cats in the sky.
Hail the felines flying by.
Make ready for the cat assault
And launch the deadly
Cat-a-pult.

RUB-A-DUB RACE

Rub-a-dub–dub!
George jumped in the tub,
And the tub got right up on its feet.

Rub-a-dub–dub!
He started to scrub,
And the tub walked out into the street.

Rub-a-dub–dark!
They jogged by the park
While George was a-washin' his face.

Rub-a-dub-dash!
They took off like a flash,
Joinin' in with a bicycle race.

Rub-a-dub–dather!
George scrubbed up a lather
And shaved off the beard on his chin.

Rub-a-dub–day!
He was bathin' away
While the tub was a-runnin' to win.

Rub-a-dub–doo!
It was time to shampoo,
And the tub started gaining some ground.

Rub-a–dub-dear!
It was really quite clear—
George's bath was the fastest in town.

Rub-a-dub–dum!
George was cleaning his bum
While the tub, it crossed over the line.

Rub-a-dub-dinse!
He finished his rinse
And said, "I believe that there trophy is mine."

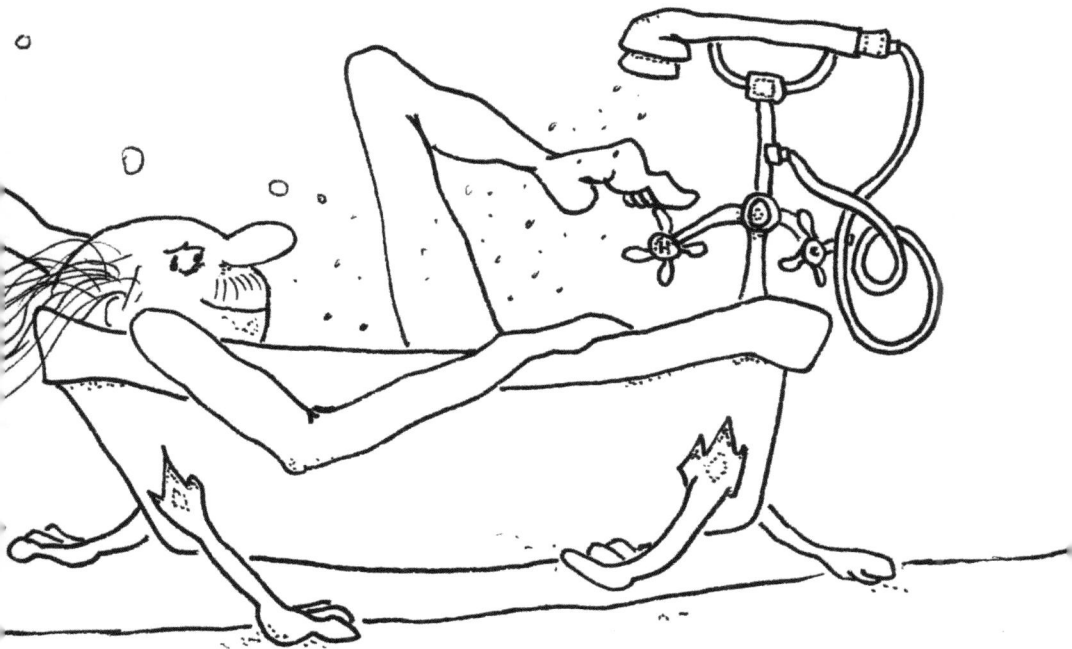

STUFFED NOSE

A turkey's just right.
A pork chop will do.
Even a bell pepper's fine for stuffin'.
But when I saw a
Nose on the menu,
I thought that for sure the chef was bluffin'.
And yet here it is,
A nose stuffed and served—
Surely among the most interesting dishes.
They say no one likes
To have a stuffed nose,
But I think it's rather delicious.

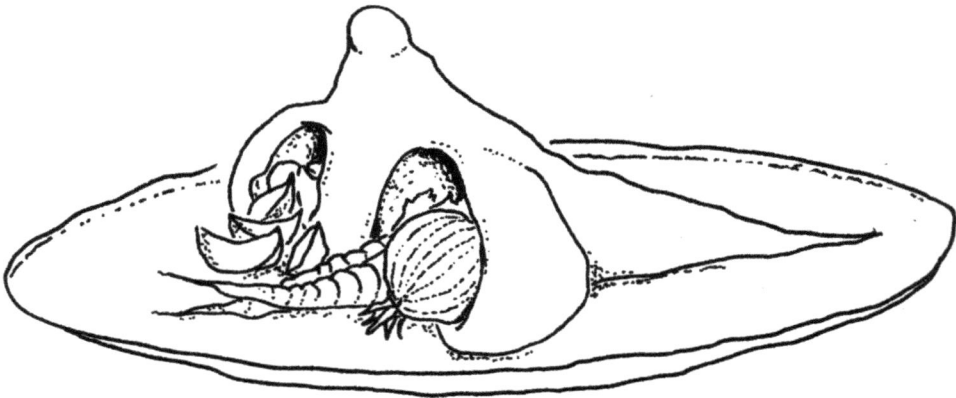

PICKLE POPSICLE

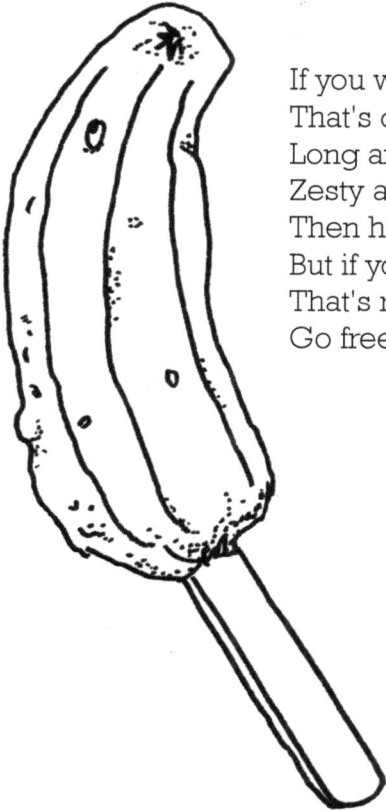

If you want something
That's crunchy and cold,
Long and green,
Zesty and bold,
Then here's a pickle popsicle to eat.
But if you want something
That's round and sweet,
Go freeze a beet.

THE KEY KEEPER

Archie McNeeses, the keeper of keys, is
A man who should smile and laugh.
With his keys he can open a lock or a safe
Or the cage of a spotted giraffe.

Archie McNeeses, the keeper of keys, is
A man who should merrily sing.
With his keys he can open a gate or a lock
Or the palace of our dear old King.

Archie McNeeses, the keeper of keys, is
A man who should happily dance.
With his keys he can start any automobile
And drive from Killarney to France.

But Archie McNeeses, the keeper of keys,
Isn't happy or merry or cheery.
He would trade all his keys
For the one key he needs
To the heart of his Marjorie dearie.

LAZY GARDENER

Perhaps I'm a tad bit lazy
With the way I tend my growin'.
Whatever springs up naturally,
I just let it keep on goin'.
Pigweed and spurge sprout all about.
The air is thick with bittersweet.
Creeping charlie crawls on the walls.
There's crabgrass growing at my feet.
The nettle gives me quite a rash.
The dandelion puffballs are nice.
Beneath this patch of nightshade lives
A family of little white mice.

This fleabane drives me insane.
The ragweed clearly makes me sneeze.
Thistles and thorns are everywhere.
The poison ivy makes me wheeze.
But I never have to rake or hoe.
I never have to plant a seed.
I simply watch my garden grow
And never ever, never ever,
Never pull a weed.

SLEEPWALKING TOM

Sleepwalking Tom walked in his sleep
Out the front door and down Maple Street,
Left on Lombardi, then a quarter a mile
Into Pete's Diner he walked with a smile.

Sleepwalking Tom talked in his sleep,
Told Mr. Pete that he wanted to eat.
Ordered a burger, then gobbled three more,
Washed them all down with a drink while he snored.

Sleepwalking Tom climbed in his sleep.
Up on the rooftop he bound with a leap.
Stood on the roof in the soft white moonlight
While the townspeople gathered to see such a sight.

Sleepwalking Tom sang in his sleep
With a sweet tenor voice that made the crowd weep.
He sang and he danced with a rapitty tap,
Wearing nothing at all but his little night cap.

BRAVEST KID

I'm the bravest kid around,
So I'm gonna walk this rope.
But just in case I trip and fall
Because my shoes are kinda small,
I'll take this handy parasol
To float me gently down.

I'm the bravest kid around.
Yes, nothin' makes me faint,
But if a sudden gusty breeze
Should make me wobble in the knees,
I'll use this jar of honeybees
To fly me to the ground.

I'm the bravest kid around.
I'll prove it here today.
But if an owl should fly the coop
And scare me with a sudden hoot,
I'll wear this handy parachute
And sail back into town.

I'm the bravest kid around,
But perhaps YOU should walk this rope,
For if I fell, the startling news
Would surely give good folks the blues
'Cause it would be a shame to lose
The bravest kid around.

FISHIN'

Down by the river,
Catfishin' with chicken liver—
Caught a shoe with a holey sole,
A bicycle tire with a big ol' hole,
A rusty pail, a baseball cap,
One red glove, a soggy map.
Reeled in an overdue library book,
A pork rind and a grappling hook,
A broken chair, an apple core,
A skateboard and a dresser drawer,
A coffee can, a diving mask,
A crumpled kite, a silver flask,
A microwave, a frying pan,
The kitchen sink, a ceiling fan,
A newspaper, a chandelier,
A whole six-pack of cold root beer,
A mustache comb, two candlesticks,
A picture frame, a bag of bricks,
A lunch box and banana peel,
A cowboy hat, a steering wheel,
A lawn mower, a license plate,
A ball of string, a roller skate.
There's lots I'm catchin', but fish I ain't.
Perhaps it's time to change my bait.

FREE RIDE

Free ride
Across the bay.
Free ride,
Just step this way.
Squeeze in tight.
Fly for free.
Travel now
In luxury!
Free ride
All this week.
Just climb on up
Into my beak.
Jump inside
For your free ride.
Free ride.
Free ride!

CHARMING AND GNIMRACH

Good Prince Charming, that lucky chap,
Woke up his gal from a magic nap
With a kiss right on the smacker,
And they lived happily ever after.

Prince Gnimrach wasn't lucky, however,
In his pursuits for a loving endeavor.
When he'd find a girl to keep
He'd kiss her lips and she'd fall asleep.

JUNGLE JIM

Jungle Jim has
Shoulders for sittin'
High up top,
A back for slidin'
Down—Kurplop!
Arms for swingin'
Back and forth,
Knees for ridin'
Like a racin' horse,
Shins for kickin'
(makes him frown),
Feet for bouncin'
Up and down,
Toes for pullin'
(makes him grin),
And hair for climbin'
Up again.

POET TREE

I sit beneath the poet tree
And wait
For a thought,
An idea,
Or some small notion
To flutter down upon my brow
And inspire me to write somehow.

JALAPEÑO NOSE

Peter picked a peck of peppers.
Then Peter picked his nose.
Then Peter, he ran quickly home
To fetch the water hose.

SOUTH POLE SANTA

The South Pole Santa is sour, they say,
And skinny and sad and shakes his fist.
He has no deer to pull his sleigh
So uses kids from the naughty list.
He goes to homes on Christmas Eve
Leaving large black lumps of coal
And sometimes snatches in their sleep
The kids who've cursed or lied or stole.
So if you're good, sleep tight tonight
And wake to presents by your tree,
But if you're naughty, quake in fright
And lock your doors
And hide with me.

TELL-A-GIRAFFE

Long before the telephone,
There was the Tell-a-giraffe,
When giraffes delivered messages
On everyone's behalf.

Folks would whisper messages,
Then the giraffes would make the rounds,
Telling what was told to them
To folks in other towns.

BLUE

Let me tell you somethin'
'Bout a lucky horse named Blue.
Never had no problems
'Cuz luck was in his shoe.

Raced a locomotive
'Cross a desert in Peru.
Beat it by a mile
'Cuz luck was in his shoe.

Went three rounds of boxing
With a champion kangaroo.
Walked away the winner
'Cuz luck was in his shoe.

Got into a shootout
With the bandit Crazy Lou.
Every bullet missed 'im
'Cuz luck was in his shoe.

Swam across a river
Of crocodiles, too.
Didn't get a single bite
'Cuz luck was in his shoe.

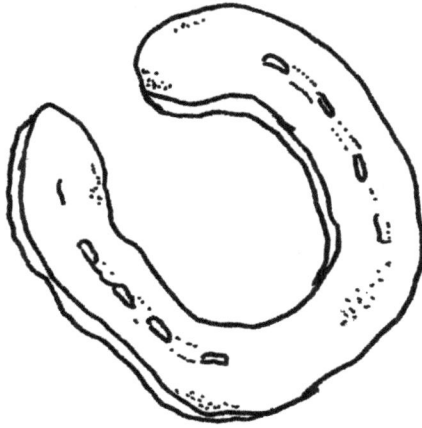

Walked into a den of snakes
Way down in Timbuktu,
Then walked right out without a scratch
'Cuz luck was in his shoe.

Jumped across the canyon grand—
Some say he even flew.
He never fell or faltered
'Cuz luck was in his shoe.

Then one day, one fateful day,
He threw his lucky shoe
While climbing up a mountain.
I swear the story's true.

He never came down from that mountain top,
That lucky horse named Blue.
He plain got stuck without no luck—
The luck was in his shoe.

LAND OF MISSING SOCKS

In the land of missing socks
You'll find red and green and blue
And pink with yellow polka dots.

You'll find skinny and long, big and wide,
And striped just like a zebra's hide.
Thick and thin, large and small,
Old and new, short and tall.
Socks of kings and socks of paupers,
Socks from drawers and socks from lockers.
Fancy, frilly, woolly, smelly socks,
Holey, sticky, crumpled, icky socks.
Socks from France and socks from Rome,
Even socks from your own home.

In the land of missing socks you'll find all varieties,
Every sock of every type and style that you please.
But in the land of missing socks,
One thing you'll never find
Is two of a kind or a pair,
Never a match or two of the same to wear.

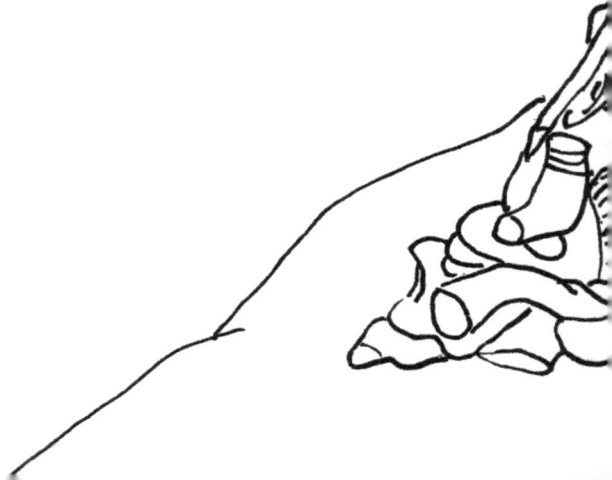

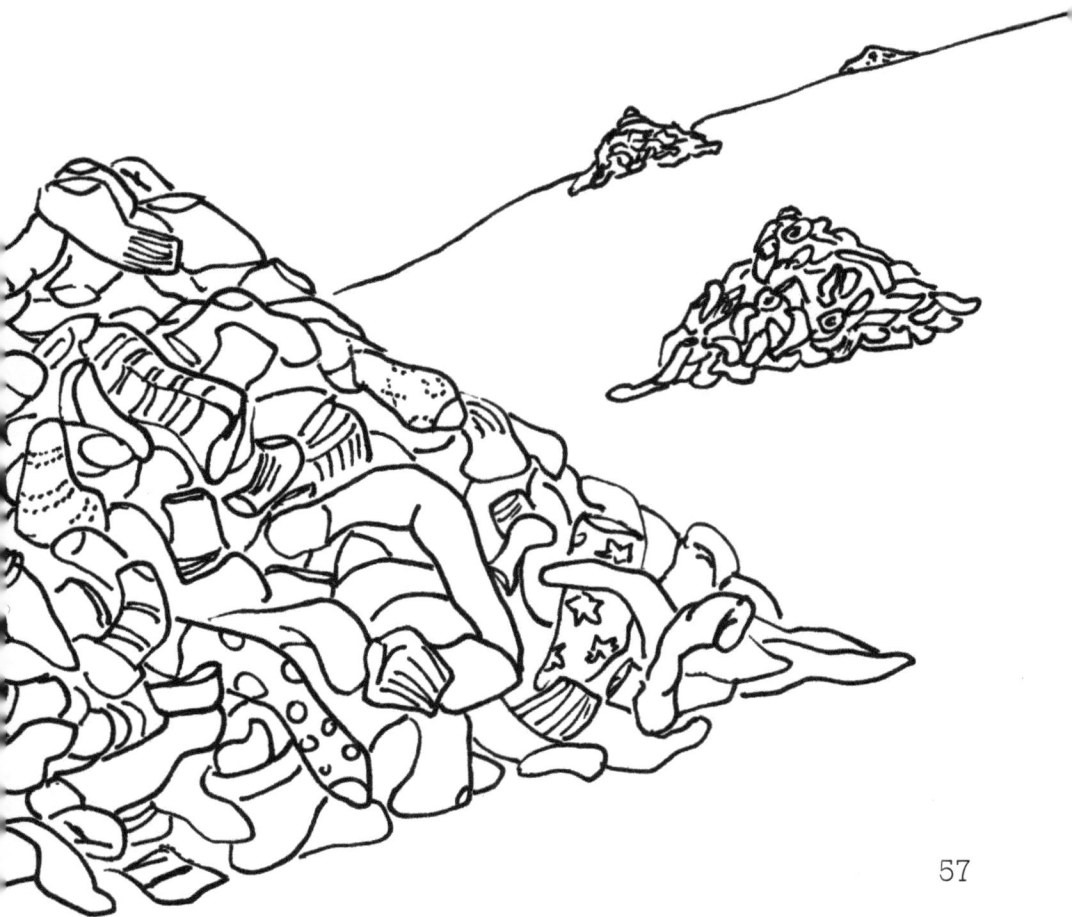

CELEBRATE

It's twelve o'clock,
Happy New Year!
Kiss me if you can.
Grab a cup of cheer.
Bang some pots and pans.
Laugh and yell and shout.
Now it twelve oh one,
Lights out!

SUNSET RIDE

His boots are burnt.
His horse is seared.
Smoke is rising from his beard.
His hat's on fire.
He singed his hide.
His saddle, spurs, and rope are fried.
His chaps are chapped;
He's not sure how—
His gunpowder just went KAPOW!
His rifle's charred.
His mess is stewed.
He smells like he's been bar-b-qued.
His bottle's dry.
His canteen's split.
He's dry as dirt, can't even spit.
His buns are smoked.
His nose is toast.
He looks a bit like cowboy roast.
Off into the sunset
Rode smokin' Jimmy Dunn.
Rode into the sunset,
And bumped into the sun.

MY BEAR CHAIR

This bear's a chair.
This chair's a bear.
I keep it in
My bear chair lair.
It sits just right,
So soft and big.
It cleans my crumbs
When I'm a pig.
It shakes itself out.
It gives me a hug.
It licks me clean
When I've been smudged.
It gently reclines.
It scratches my back.
It follows me 'round
And carries my pack.
Yes, my bear chair's there
Any time I need it,
But I must remember
To trim its claws
And never forget to feed it!

WITCH'S BREW

Drink this tasty witch's brew.
It's sure to give you déjà vu.

WITCH'S BREW

Drink this tasty witch's brew.
It's sure to give you déjà vu.

WRITER'S BLOCK

Everyone has a poem or two
Buried deep inside,
Somewhere in their head,
Where good poems like to hide.
Some can think 'em out.
Some can sing 'em out.
Some just need to close
Their eyes and shout.
But if that doesn't work,
You, my friend, are in luck.
I can get your poems out
Even when they're stuck!

GOLDEN TREASURE

We found it!
We found it!
The treasure is ours.
We'll buy spotted ponies,
Airplanes, and cars.
We'll travel the world
From Havana to Spain.
We'll eat all the best foods,
Like French dip and chow mein.
We'll spend all our money
Until we grow old.
Now let's open this chest
And divide up our...
Bananas?

DREAMER

I found an old dusty dream
Put away long ago in some forgotten place.
I scrubbed and polished and shined it
Until I could see the reflection
Of an old familiar face
Smiling at a forgotten dream made new again.

MUSIC INSIDE

There's music inside that ol' clock tower.
But, oh, would you look at the time?
I don't feel like waiting for hours
To hear that ol' clock tower chime.
So I'll bounce
And I'll pull
And I'll tug
At those hands,
Twirling them 'round and 'round.
Perhaps the day will go faster that way,
And that clock tower's music will sound.

MIDNIGHT

You should be home asleep in your bed
When the clock strikes twelve,
When the good fairy's magic ends
And the mischief of goblins and ghouls begins,
When the werewolf's howl echoes
Through the dark of night,
And a black silhouette
Crosses the moon in flight.

You should be home asleep in your bed
When the clock strikes twelve,
But you will be here with me instead
To see what wonders 'round us roam
Late at night.
Away from home.
When the clock strikes twelve.

JACKIE-O

Jackie-o is happy-o
Except on Halloween,
When other children tease him
And treat him cruel and mean.
They smash him.
They bash him.
They blow his candle out.
They point their fingers at his face.
They laugh and scream and shout.
They stuff their wrappers in his ears
And roll him down the street.
That's why he's always hiding
When you go trick or treat.

TEACHER'S PET

Pretty Miss Porter,
Her students adored her.
They brought her sweet apples to eat.
An apple from Amy,
An apple from Johnny,
An apple from Katie and Pete.
An apple from Carrie,
An apple from Harry,
An apple from Scotty,
An apple from Sherry,
An apple from Joey,
An apple from Chloe,
An apple from Sally and Chris.
When kind little Fred
Brought a banana instead,
She smiled and gave him a kiss!

THE MYNAH BIRD

Can you hear
    Can you hear

The mynah bird
    The mynah bird

Repeat the sound
    Repeat the sound

Of every word?
    Of every word?

The problem is
    The problem is

He will not stop
    He will not stop

And all he does
    And all he does

Is talk, talk, talk!
    Is talk, talk, talk!

Let's go to lunch,
    Let's go to lunch,

You and I,
    You and I,

And order us
    And order us

Some mynah pie...

TOO MUCH TO DO

"Hey there, little one passing by,
Will you please help hold up the sky
So I can rest for just a bit
And stretch my achin' back?"

"I should, I could, I would for you,
But I have other things to do.
I must deliver right away
These apples in my sack.

"And then I must brush down the mule
And shear the sheep
And spin the wool
And polish the brass
And feed the bull
And clean the stalls
And go to school.

"Yes, I'm as busy as can be.
There's just too much to do, you see,
So you're just gonna have to keep
That sky upon your back."

MAMA SAID

Mama said,
"Keep your feet on the ground,
Firmly planted,
Safe and sound,
And you will grow up proud and tall."

But that's not what I want at all.

"Then stuck in the clouds
Your head will be,
With your feet in the air,"
She said to me.
"And go where e'er the wind may blow."

Dear mama, how I'll miss you so . . .

ECHOES

Somewhere deep beneath the ground,
Underneath the hills and roads,
A cave of echoes can be found,
And there each faded echo goes.
Each call of love, each shout of joy,
Each startled cry from girls and boys,
Sounds of laughter, sounds of fright,
Screams of torture in the night.
Marching orders, battle cries,
Screeching eagles flying by,
Bugles sounding, freedom ringing,
Pirate cannons, mermaids singing.
The trumpeting of elephants,
Operas sung in eloquence,
Yodels from the mountain highlands,
Tribal chants from distant islands.
Heehaws from old stubborn mules,
Moanings of great ghastly ghouls,
Yeehaws from the Wild West,
The creakings of old sea chests.
Songs of victors' glorious words,
Now just whispers Barley heard.
But when all is silent,
When all is still,
Listen.
Listen,
And you will
Hear the faded sounds below,
Deep beneath the hills and roads
In the cave of echoes.

SAM AND SALLY

There once was a man
Named Whistlin' Sam
Who whistled in a one-man band.
He spent night and day
Just whistlin' away.
His whistlin' was really quite grand.

There once lived a gal
Called Whistlin' Sal
Who whistled just like a canary.
Her favorite pastime
Was whistlin' a chime.
She whistled to make herself merry.

When Sam and Sal met,
They made a duet
And whistled a love song together.
Now wooed and wed, they're
A whistlin' pair,
And they'll whistle sweet music forever.

PICK A MASK

Hairgsy, scargsy, spoogsy, bad.
Heftily, hungrily, happily, mad.
Happzy, snappzy, quackzy, sad.
Bumpily, grumpily, slumpily, glad.
Picks a mask and puts it on—
Takes it home and shows your mom!

83

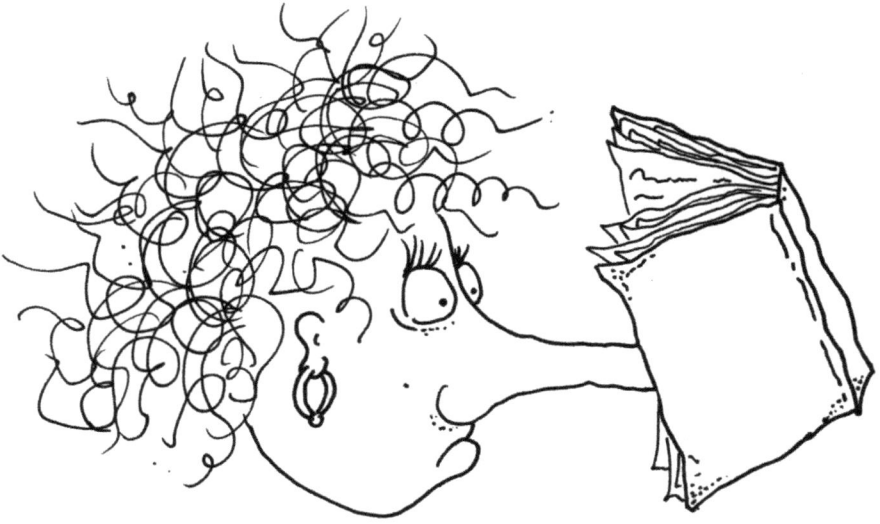

STUCK

Ashley Lou stuck her nose in a book
And wouldn't you know,
She couldn't get it out.
So everywhere she'd go,
She'd read all about
A dragon's flight
And a princess of course,
And a daring knight
On his trusty white horse.
But golly gee and fiddle,
Although the story was splendid,
With her nose stuck in the middle,
She never knew how it ended.

THE MAGIC HEN

Charlie Gruel stoled the hen
That laid the golden egg.

But Charlie Gruel was cruel.
"Lay!" he said,
And the hen laid.

The hen laid a pink egg.
The hen laid a blue.
The hen laid a green
And a purple one too.
Then spotted white
And speckled brown,
And Charlie Gruel began to frown.

"Lay!" he said,
And the hen laid.
But Charlie Gruel was sore dismayed,

For since he stoled that magic hen,
She's never laid a gold again.

ATHLETES' FEET

I have a case of athletes' feet.
Oh, whatever shall I do?
A box filled up with athletes' feet,
But not a single shoe.
They smell quite sour and, what's more,
I think they're turning blue.
Ma says I should shine them
Until they look like new.
Coach says I should run them
Until they're tried and true.
The doc says I should cover them
With purple slimy goo.
Perhaps I'll get some cages
And start a feet foot zoo.
Or clean them with some feet soap
And maybe sell a few.
Or boil one up in a pot
To make athlete's foot stew.
I've tried to find an athlete
To give 'em one or two,
But no one wants an athlete's foot—
How 'bout you?

SCRATCH 'N' SNIFF

He don't bathe; he don't bother
To wash or to lather.
They call him the scratch-and-sniff lad.
Just scratch and then sniff,
And you'll get a good whiff
Of somethin'—
Could be good,
Could be bad.
Scratch an ear,
Smells like root beer.
Scratch his head,
Smells like sweet bread.
Scratch his belly,
Smells like grape jelly.
Scratch his bum,
Smells like rum.
Scratch his back,
That's potato sack.
His elbows and knees
Smell like carrots and peas,
And his nose smells like
Corn from the farm.
But don't scratch his feet
(Unless you like rotten meat),
And never scratch under his arm!

AN EXTRA HAND

Everyone says it would be grand
To have a handy extra hand.
But three-handed Fritz,
He thinks it's the pits.
You have to understand
That when he sits,
The sit he sits
Is really a one-handed handstand.

ZOMBIE ZED

My best friend is Zombie Zed.
It doesn't matter that he's dead;
We're as close as friends can be,
Me and Zed,
Zed and me.
He says, "Let's play."
I say, "Okay!"
He says, "Let's run."
I say, "Sounds fun."
He says, "Tag, now you're it!"
Then I chase him 'round a bit.
He says, "Let's have a rest."
I say, "Zed, you know best."
He says, "I think it's time to eat."
Then I go running down the street.
(He is a zombie, after all!)

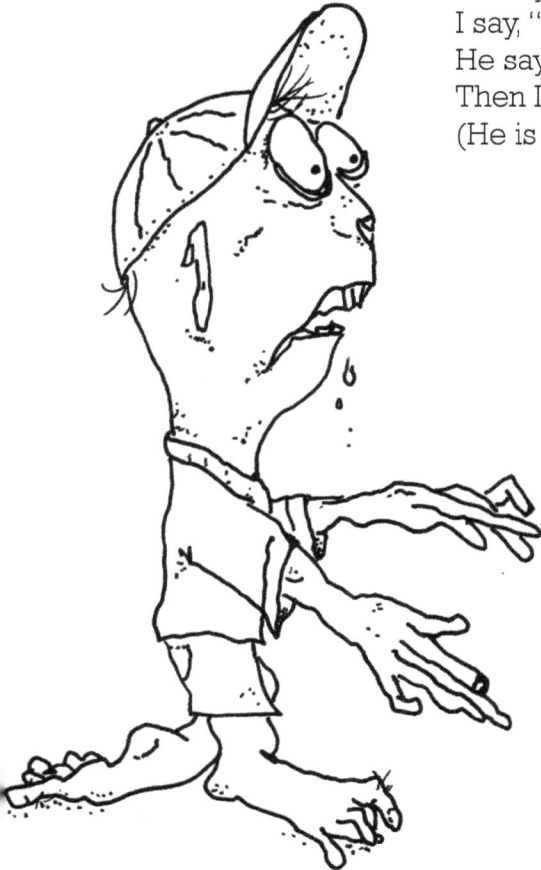

SHOOTIN' STARS

Cowboy Bill
Got a thrill
By shootin' down the stars.

But too much fun
With his smokin' gun
Put Billy behind bars.

Now if you spy
Up in the sky
A star that's tumblin' down,

Then there's no doubt:
Bill's busted out
And shootin' up the town.

WHAT TO DO IF THE GOBBLEY-GOO COMES FOR YOU

Scream!
Cry!
Call out for help!
Hold on to your teddy and let out a yelp.
Tuck in your toes and run to your mother
And snuggle down deep in her warm fuzzy covers.
But do not just lay there asleep in your sheets—
You know what the Gobbley-Goo monster eats!

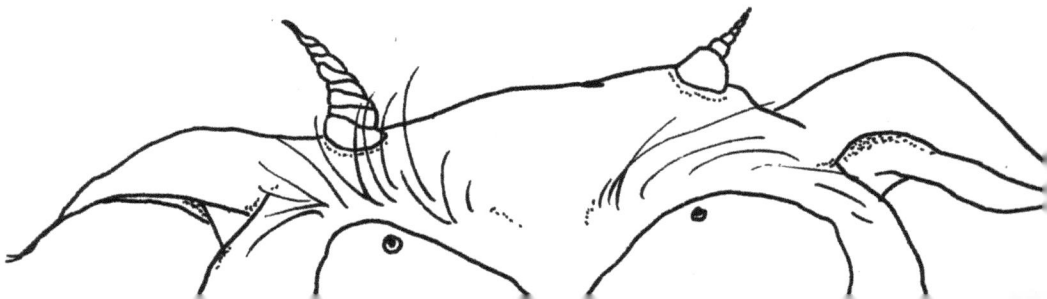

CONTEST

First we'll have a staring contest
To find out who will blink.
Then we'll have a smelling contest
To see who has more stink.
Then we'll have an eating contest
With fish 'n' chips 'n' pie.
Then we'll climb a crow's nest
And try to touch the sky.
Then we'll spin and spin around
To see who will fall down.
Then we'll try and find just who
Can make the grossest sound.
Then whoever does the best,
It's them that gets to win
And gets to start all over
And do it all again.

FIT

I throw a fit—
I scream and whine.
I moan and make a mess
When my mother says to me,
"It's time to get you dressed."

CAVE MAN

Ed was just a cave man,
Did what cave men do.
Carried 'round a wooden club,
Never wore a shoe,
Lived inside a simple cave,
Slept on a slab of rock,
Liked to draw things on his wall,
Almost never talked.
Then one day the cave man Ed
Met a nice cave lady.
They shared his cave and his stone bed.
Then came a small cave baby,
Then three more (that made four).
In total they were six,
Six cave people plus a dog
Who liked to fetch cave sticks.
And every day the children played,
Biting and clubbing each other.
The small cave girl would snarl and growl
And hit her three cave brothers.
Then the whole cave family
Would rumble 'round so loud,
And Ed would grunt,
"Ugh ugh ugh ugh,"
Because he was so proud.

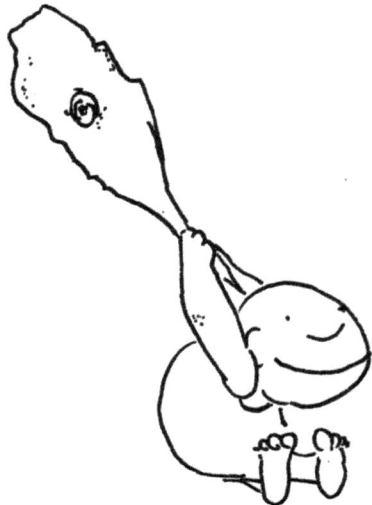

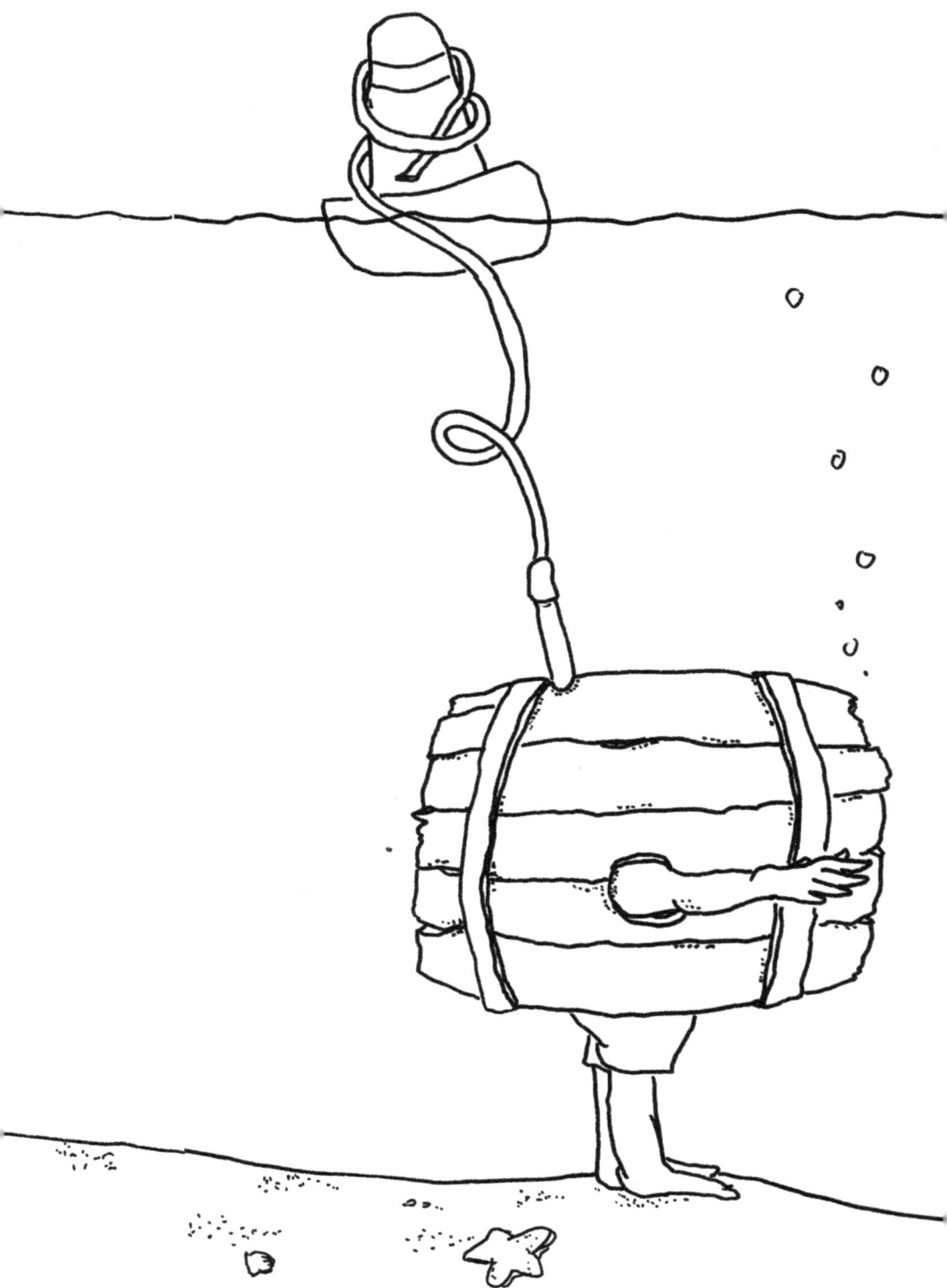

HOMEMADE SUBMARINE

My homemade submarine,
My homemade submarine—
I dove into the deep blue sea
To see what could be seen
But forgot to put a window in
My homemade submarine.

Oh what would I have seen?
Oh what would I have seen?
A shark, a shell, a fish, a whale?
A seaweed garden green?
How I wish I had a window in
My homemade submarine!

SEA SHELLS

They say that you'll hear blowing wind
And waves upon the sand
And distant sounds of ocean birds
And cries of fishermen.
But all I heard when I placed
A seashell to my ear
Was a great
Big
SNAP!

BANANA PHONE

If you hear this banana ring,
Pick it up and have a yak.
If no one cares to talk today,
Have a yummy yellow snack.
But if you spend too long waiting
For that friend to make a call,
The flies will take your phone away,
And you'll have no snack at all.

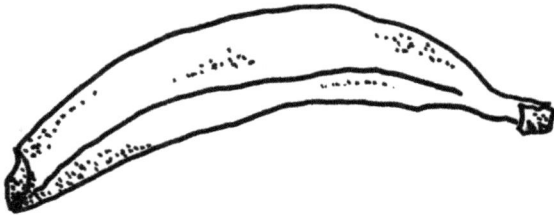

SLY THE TIE GUY

Sly McFly learned to tie a tie
But never to a tie untie.
So every time a tie he wore,
He wore that tie forevermore,
Until his neck was full of ties—
A thousand ties on Sly McFly.

Then one day a strange wind blew,
Carrying a strange tune.

So Sly McFly began to dance
And leap and spin
And run and prance.
And all those ties wavin' round
Lifted Sly up off the ground.
Away he went soaring high
With his ties into the sky.

That's the day the people say
That Sly McFly done flew away.

UnMake It
FREE

ReMake It 5¢

102

UNMAKE-IT MACHINE

Unmake-it machine!
Unmake-it machine!
Try the amazing unmake-it machine!
Bring me your baseballs—
I'll turn them to string.
I'll ungrow your flowers
Back into spring.
This small, spoiled prince
Was a tyrannical king
Before the amazing unmake-it machine.

Bring a cake to unbake
Or a song to unsing.
Yes, this fat caterpillar
Was a butterfly wing,
And this lump of black coal
Was a bright diamond ring
Before they went through
The unmake-it machine.
So come right this way;
You can bring anything
And try the amazing unmake-it machine.

RUNNING AWAY

The dish ran away with the spoon
And, oh, what a stir they made.
Because of their escapade
My kitchen's a big charade:
The butcher block left town with the clock.
My muffin tin's gone missing.
The nutcracker and ice cream scoop
Were seen secretly kissing.
The garlic press and pizza cutter
Appear to be in love.
The frying pan eloped
With my favorite oven glove.

And who knew the cork screw
Had a crush on the rolling pin?
The spatula and funnel
I may never see again.
The poultry shears skipped town
With my very best cheese shredder.
The ladle and the can opener
Wrote a lengthy goodbye letter.

So I'll just sit here,
Sad and lonely
On the kitchen floor
Because I don't have anyone
To cook with any more.

LOUD MOUTH SUE

There once was a girl called Loud Mouth Sue
Who wouldn't listen but loved to talk
(Almost as much as you).
She wouldn't listen to her ma.
She wouldn't listen to her pa.
She wouldn't listen to her teacher
Or her preacher or grandpa.
She wouldn't listen to the doctor
Or the dentist or the fireman
Or the lifeguard at the pool
Or anyone at school, especially the librarian.
But she talked the live long day.
She talked about her fingernails.
She talked about department sales.
She talked about most everything,
Like diamond rings in great detail.
She talked about her lovely clothes.
She talked about her dainty nose.
She talked about her hobbies too,
Like how she grew a summer rose.
But she would never ever listen.
And all that talking and not listening
Grew her mouth and shrunk her ears
Until she could no longer hear.
That's what happened to Loud Mouth Sue.
But I'm sure YOU have nothing to fear.
(Now what was that you were saying?)

MOUNTAIN MOVERS

Throwing rocks,
Heaving boulders,
Crashing slabs like thunder.
Through the night
The giants work
A feat of wondrous wonder.
Rumbling tumbling
Shakes the ground,
Loud and proud and violent
Until the day breaks from the night
And everything falls silent.
Now see where once a mountain stood
There lies a flatland prairie,
And here a mighty mountain stands
Where once there was a valley.

CROCOSMILE

"I'm going to surf a while,"
He said.

"On that long green crocodile,"
He said.

"The one with the crooked smile,"
He said.

Then down the winding Nile
Went Ted,

Down a mile, around the bend,
Having fun and hangin' ten,

Never to be seen again.

HELPING HAND

Here's a helping hand for you
To help you with your chores and such.
I would have given you more than just a hand,
But a whole helping person just costs too much.

JUNGLE VINE

A jungle vine is a fine place to be
Swingin' up high in a jungle tree,
Swingin' way up through the jungle air,
Swingin' and sayin' a hopeful prayer
That the angry hippos, pointy rhinos,
Slinking snakes and crocodiles,
Man-eating cats, poison frogs,
Elephants and mad warthogs
Cannot reach me swingin' there.

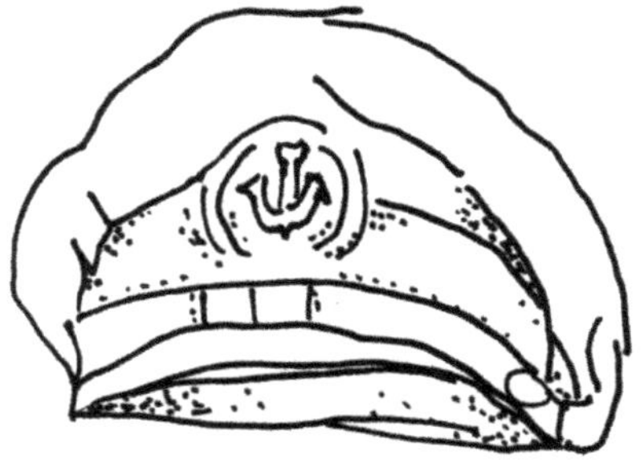

TOP TO BOTTOM

Said the captain's boots to the captain's hat,
"I envy your station there.
You gaze upon the rolling waves
Across the open seas,
High atop the captain's head,
Amid the salty breeze."

Said the captain's hat to the captain's boots,
"How lucky you must feel
To walk and run and climb about
And lead the men in chase
And dance a lively sailor's jig
Each time the fiddle plays."

HAIR GROW

"Hair Grow," the bottle read.
"Apply to the chin,
The chest, or the head."
But I can't read—
Oh, what dread!
I tipped the bottle
And drank it instead.

PEANUT BUTTER MAGIC

Peanut butter stops a squeaky
Wagon wheel from squeaking.
Peanut butter stops a rusty
Water pail from leaking.
Peanut butter works real nice
At catching little furry mice
And getting gum unstuck from hair
And baking cookies for the fair
And making other people stare
(When you wear it on your nose)
And gluing broken wooden toys
And bribing other girls and boys
And stopping angry barking dogs
From making too much noise.
Then if there is any left,
The best thing you can do is spread
A great big glob of peanut butter
On a slice of homemade bread
And eat a peanut butter sandwich.

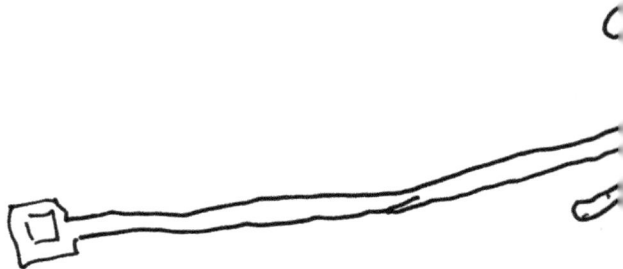

JELLY

The only thing to do with jelly
Is put it in a hungry belly.

CHOICES

Sometimes you're on top,
Smilin' happy,
Feelin' bright.

Sometimes you're on bottom,
Feelin' life's just
Not quite right.

But usually you're in the middle,
Not quite happy,
Not quite sad.

So choose to smile.
Choose to laugh.
You'll find your choices
Make you glad.

LITTLE PIGGIES

This little piggy went to market
To buy a loaf of bread.
This little piggy stayed home
And jumped upon her bed.
This little piggy had roast beef
And sweet potato gravy.
This little piggy had none
So went and joined the navy.
And this little piggy cried, "Wee wee wee,"
While skipping in the rain
Then splished and splashed
And splooshed and sploshed
All the way home again.

A-ROLLIN'

Ground's a-spinnin'.
Sky's a-turnin'.
Houses goin' round and round.
People a-circlin'.
Trees a-bouncin'.
World is movin' up and down.
All the things around me
Become a splendid thrill
When I am a-rollin'
In a tire down the hill.

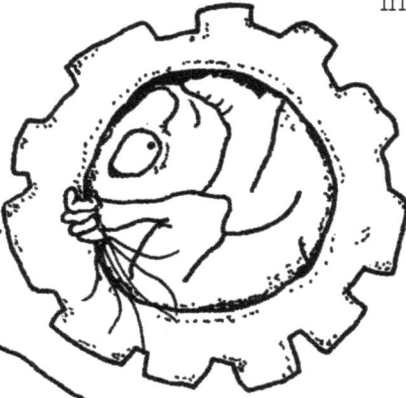

HOGWASH

Hogwash,
Hogwash.
Not a cat or dog wash.
Come and fill a water pail.
Scrub your hog from head to tail.
Rinse him down with buttermilk.
Pat him dry with woven silk.
Shine his snout. Swab his ears.
Sprinkle powder on his rears.
Brush his teeth with piggy paste.
Hurry! There's no time to waste.
Feed him corn and apples too.
Scent him with a rose perfume.
Almost ready for the day!
Mr. Butcher's on his way.
What's that?
What's that I hear you say?
You'll bathe your hog in mud today?
Well . . . okay.

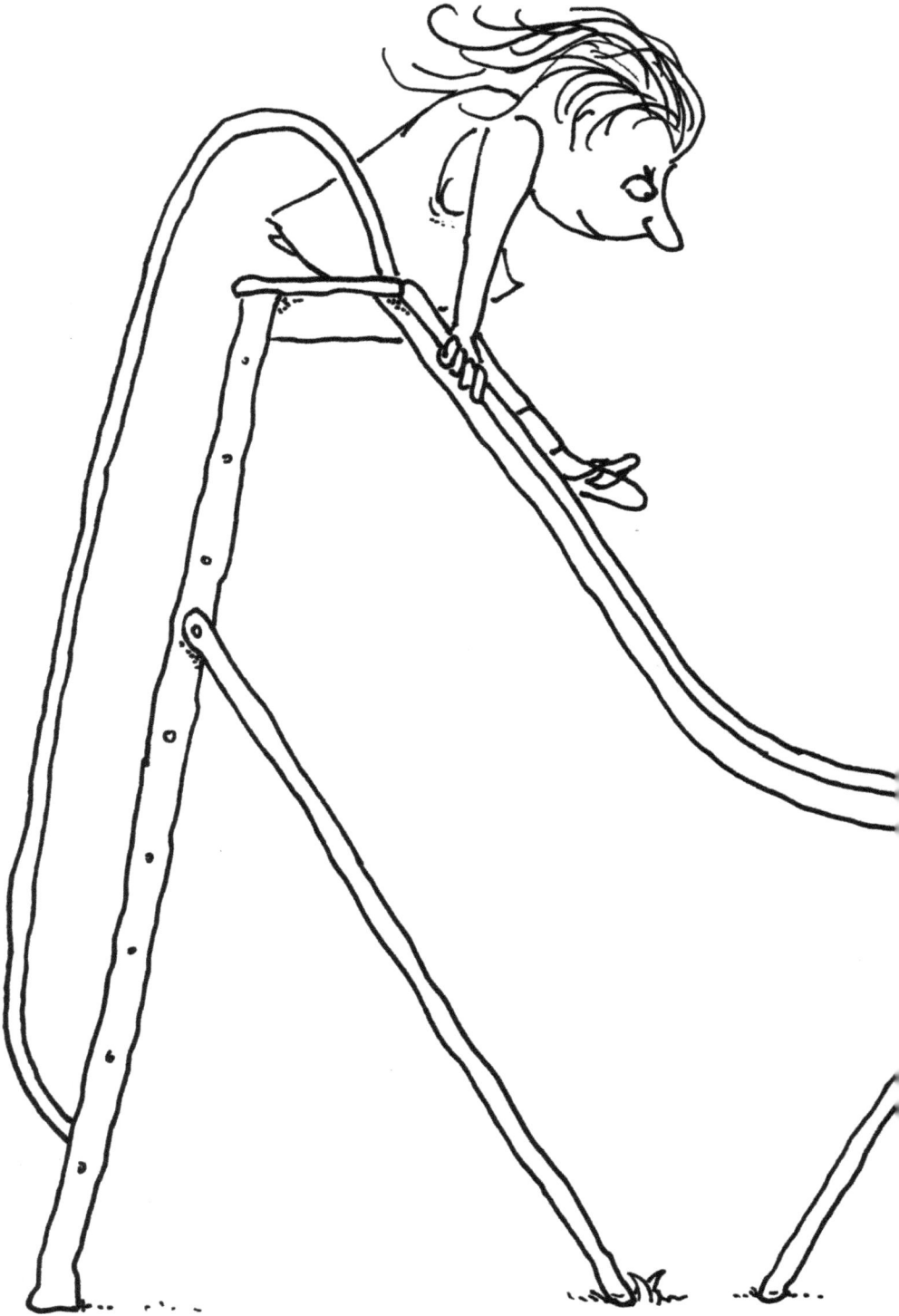

SLIDE

Go down the slide;
Enjoy the ride.
Go up the slide;
Get a foot in the eye.

GOOSED

There is an old woman
Who loves to pinch bums.
She'll grab and squeeze tight
'Tween her fingers and thumbs.
If you suddenly feel
A pinch on your hide,
More likely than not,
She's just goosed your backside.

PET PEEVE

Poor Missus Mattie McCleave
Couldn't get rid of a nasty pet peeve.
Even when Mattie would weep and grieve,
That pet peeve
Wouldn't leave.

She tried to correct it and scold it,
To teach it and preach it and mold it,
Even to pet it and hold it.
But that pet peeve
Still wouldn't leave.

It burped when she tried to talk.
It nipped at her heels when she tried to walk.
So Mattie tried electric shock,
But that pet peeve
Still wouldn't leave.

She got down on her knees
And did her best to beg and to plead,
"Oh please, oh please,
Oh please, please, please!"
But that pet peeve
Still wouldn't leave.

So Missus Mattie McCleave
Kept and adopted that nasty pet peeve
And bathed it and pressed it
And combed it and dressed it
And loved it and named it Steve.

THE KISS THAT MISSED

From high up in her tower
A princess blew a lovely kiss
For her prince to catch and keep,
But when he stretched and leaped, he missed.

And their love grew cold and dreary,
And they never wooed or married
All because of the kiss that missed.

But the kiss that missed kept goin'
And blew into the town
Where a wee baby was cryin'
And her mother wore a frown.

And the baby giggled and cooed,
Putting mother in a good mood
All because of the kiss that missed.

Then the kiss that missed flew on
To a land so barren and dry
That nothing would grow
And never was seen a cloud up in the sky.

And the rains began to shower,
And the fields grew lovely flowers
All because of the kiss that missed.

When people saw the kiss that missed,
They always stopped and smiled,
For no one in the land had seen
A kiss like that in a while.

And everyone frolicked and danced
While happily lovers romanced,
All because of the kiss that missed.

Then one day the kiss sailed away
On a westward ocean breeze,
Passing a crew of sailors caught
In a storm upon the seas.

And the sailors sang so merry,
For no longer were they weary,
All because of the kiss that missed.

If you don't believe my tale
I will have to beg your pardon,
For when the kiss that missed landed here,
Gently in my garden,
I caught it with my catching net
And haven't even shared it yet.

Come take a closer look, my love,
And I'll give you the kiss that missed.

PAPER EATER

Someone saw a paper eater
In the neighborhood
Lookin' for a scrap to eat.
So I think we should
Hide the books and magazines
Underneath the bed;
Get my birth certificate
Closed up in the shed;
Lock up my paper airplanes,
My drawings and my poems—
Don't leave out the photographs;
Paper proof our home!
Put my favorite stickers
Way up in a tree.
Place my love notes in a bottle
Floating out to sea.
Bury the origami
Safely in the yard.
Stamp and mail away the letters.
Hire a paper guard.
My music sheet, dollar bills,
And baseball card collection
Need to be secured
With maximum protection.
So if the monster asks for paper,
Tell 'im we're not able.
But if you have to give it somethin',
My report card's on the table.

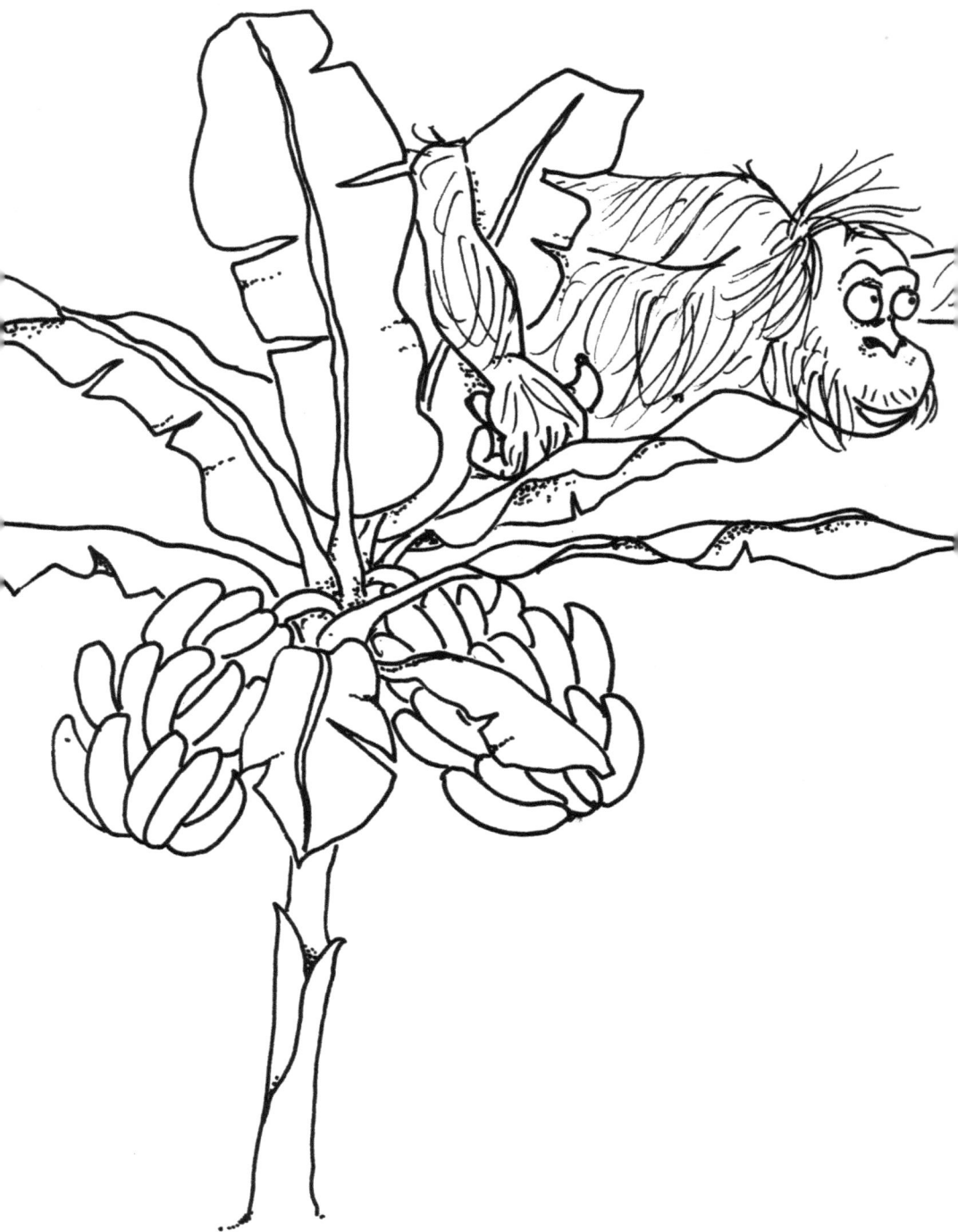

FLYING BANANAS

The orangutan threw his bananarang.
Tra la la la lee!
It whirled and twirled and looped around
And flew back to his tree.

I threw my yellow banana too.
Tra la la la loo!
It whirled and twirled and looped around
And SPLAT!—covered me in goo.

IRISES

Watch the irises.
(It's important that you do.)
I'm pretty sure
Theyz watchin' you.

LETTY SPAGHETTI

Where, oh where, is the long golden hair
Of beautiful Letty LeFlair?
It was there after breakfast this morning
When she nibbled on eggs and toast.
It was there after midday lunch
When she gobbled potatoes and roast.
But when she dined this evening
Something went terribly wrong,
For after dear Letty
Slurped up her spaghetti,
Her hair was mysteriously gone.

FOOTPRINTS

Someone's been this way before,
On this strange and broken trail.
I can see their footprints on the valley floor
And upon the mountain tops where eagles soar,
Leading through the forest to the ocean shore,
Inviting us to follow and explore.
Oh, what a tale they tell.

STICKY SITUATION

I gave this goat my bubble gum.
Now I'm in big trouble!
How was I supposed to know
A goat could blow a bubble?

MOON BOAT

Come with me in my moon boat
Across the starry night,
To the place where dreams dance free
And wild thoughts take flight.

Come with me in my moon boat.
We'll sail the azure skies—
Or save the fare and meet me there
When you close your eyes.

INDEX

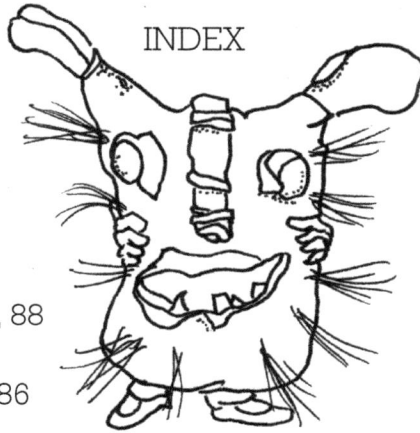

An Extra Hand, 88
A-Rollin', 122
Athletes' Feet, 86

Banana Phone, 99
Blue, 54
Bravest Kid, 45

Cambridge Court, 18
Camouflage Jack, 28
Cat-A-Pult, 33
Cave Man, 94
Celebrate, 58
Charming and Gnimrach, 48
Chimney Town, 25
Choices, 119
Contest, 93
Crocosmile, 110

Dirt Bug Doug, 30
Dreamer, 67

Echoes, 78

Fishin', 46
Fit, 93
Flying Bananas, 133
Footprints, 136
Free Ride, 47
Fuddle Puddle, 21

Golden Treasure, 66
Gooberries, 15
Goosed, 126

Hair Grow, 115
Helping Hand, 111
Hogwash, 123
Homemade Submarine, 97
Honey Bear, 20
Hungry Couch, 10

I've Never Ever, 32
Irises, 134

Jackie-O, 73
Jalapeno Nose, 50
Jelly, 118
Johnny Appleseed, 27
Jungle Jim, 49
Jungle Vine, 113

Land of Missing Socks, 56
Lazy Gardener, 40
Letty Spaghetti, 135
Little Piggies, 120
Loud Mouth Sue, 106

Mama Said, 77
Midnight, 71
Missing Monster, 23
Moon Boat, 138
Mountain Movers, 108
Music Inside, 68
My Bear Chair, 62

Paper Eater, 130
Peanut Butter Magic, 116
Pet Peeve, 127
Pick a Mask, 82
Pickle Popsicle, 37
Pickpocket, 8
Poet Tree, 50

Rainbow in a Bottle, 15
Ready, Set, Go!, 9
Remember, 7
Rub-a-Dub Race, 34
Running Away, 104

Sam and Sally, 80
Scissors, 16
Scratch 'n' Sniff, 87
Sea Shells, 98
Shootin' Stars, 90
Sleepwalking Tom, 42
Slide, 125
Sly the Tie Guy, 100

South Pole Santa, 51
Sticky Situation, 137
Stuck, 84
Stuffed Nose, 36
Sunset Ride, 61

Teacher's Pet, 74
Tell-a-Giraffe, 53
The Key Keeper, 38
The King with
    a Paper Crown, 13
The Kiss That Missed, 128
The Magic Hen, 85
The Mynah Bird, 75
Too Much to Do, 76
Top to Bottom, 114

Unmake-it Machine, 103

What to do
    if the Gobbley-Goo
    Comes for You, 92
Wishes, 12
Witch's Brew, 63
Witch's Brew, 64
Working, 22
Writer's Block, 65

Zombie Zed, 89

For their support and encouragement in the making of this book, thank you Kimberly, Kristina, Mark, Gwen, and George.

To the artists and authors whose works I have enjoyed throughout my life and who have in many ways been my teachers: Bill Peet, Ogden Nash, Beatrix Potter, Maurice Sendak, Betty MacDonald, Arnold Lobel, Mercer Mayer, and of course Shel Silverstein—thank you.

Each of you has influenced my work in some way small or great.

Ken

www.ingramcontent.com/pod-product-compliance
Lightning Source LLC
Chambersburg PA
CBHW041829090426
42811CB00038B/2363/J